MW01154189

Lerner SPORTS

TIM DUNCAN
POWER FORWARD

PERCY LEED

LERNER PUBLICATIONS ◆ MINNEAPOLIS

Lerner Publications Company
An imprint of Lerner Publishing Group, Inc.
241 First Avenue North
Minneapolis, MN 55401 USA

For reading levels and more information, look up this title at www.lernerbooks.com.

Main body text set in Myriad Pro Semibold.
Typeface provided by Adobe.

Editor: Alison Lorenz **Photo Editor:** Brianna Kaiser

Library of Congress Cataloging-in-Publication Data

Names: Leed, Percy, 1968– author.
Title: Tim Duncan : power forward / Percy Leed.
Description: Minneapolis, MN : Lerner Publications, 2022. | Series: Epic Sports Bios (Lerner™ Sports) | Includes bibliographical references and index. | Audience: Ages 7–11 | Audience: Grades 4–6 | Summary: "Tim Duncan trained to be an Olympic swimmer before beginning to play basketball at 14. Follow the star forward from his home in the Virgin Islands to the top of the NBA and beyond"— Provided by publisher.
Identifiers: LCCN 2019055036 (print) | LCCN 2019055037 (ebook) | ISBN 9781728414706 (library binding) | ISBN 9781728414805 (paperback) | ISBN 9781728414812 (ebook)
Subjects: LCSH: Duncan, Tim, 1976- —Juvenile literature. | Basketball players—United States—Biography—Juvenile literature.
Classification: LCC GV884.D86 L44 2021 (print) | LCC GV884.D86 (ebook) | DDC 796.323092 [B]—dc23

LC record available at https://lccn.loc.gov/2019055036
LC ebook record available at https://lccn.loc.gov/2019055037

Manufactured in the United States of America
1-48651-49074-12/30/2020

TABLE OF CONTENTS

SLAM DUNCAN

It was Game 5 of the 1999 National Basketball Association (NBA) Finals. Power forward Tim Duncan and the rest of the San Antonio Spurs were hoping to lock down the championship. The Spurs had already won three games in the series. One more would seal the deal.

Tim Duncan dribbles during a game in 1999.

FACTS AT A GLANCE

Date of birth: April 25, 1976

Position: power forward

League: NBA

Personal highlights: grew up in the US
Virgin Islands; pursued Olympic swimming
before switching to basketball; earned a
degree in psychology; became a coach for the
Spurs after retiring

Professional highlights: won NBA Rookie
of the Year; led the Spurs to five NBA
championships; earned Finals Most Valuable
Player (MVP) three times; won league MVP
two times

Duncan blocks a shot from Latrell Sprewell in Game 1 of the 1999 NBA Finals.

The Knicks' Latrell Sprewell helped New York jump to an early lead of 21–15. Duncan fought back. He brought the Spurs to within one point of the Knicks by the start of the second quarter. He sat down for a short rest. But as soon as he did, the Knicks went wild. New York led by eight points when Duncan returned to the court.

The game became a duel between Duncan and Sprewell. The two players traded baskets, each more impressive than the last. With three minutes left in the game, the Knicks led 77–75. Sprewell took a shot and missed. Duncan made a foul shot, cutting the Knicks' lead to one.

Then Spurs point guard Avery Johnson made a perfect two-pointer. With two seconds left, Sprewell charged the basket. But Duncan got there first. He and Spurs captain David Robinson defended the basket, and Sprewell missed his final shot. The buzzer blared, and Duncan and the Spurs claimed their first NBA title.

(*From left:*) Duncan and teammates Antonio Daniels, Gerard King, Sean Elliott, and Avery Johnson celebrate their Finals victory.

SERIOUS SWIMMER

Timothy Duncan was born on April 25, 1976, on St. Croix, one of the US Virgin Islands. Tim was the baby of the family. His parents and his older sisters, Cheryl and Tricia, adored him.

From the time he was very young, Tim looked up to his sisters. It wasn't long before he followed in their footsteps and joined the family sport: swimming.

The Olympic torch at the 1988 Olympic Games

Swimming was more than a hobby for the Duncan girls. As a teenager, Tricia earned a spot swimming backstroke on the 1988 US Virgin Islands Olympic team. Tim was full of pride for his sister. He couldn't wait for his chance to compete for his homeland.

By the time he was 13, Tim had set records in St. Croix for both the 50-meter and 100-meter freestyle. Everyone was convinced he would be on the 1992 Olympic team. Ione, Tim's mother, took night shifts at her job so she could cheer on the kids at their swim meets. "She was my biggest fan," Tim said later. "Every meet, she was the loudest parent there."

But life took an unexpected turn. The Duncan family suffered two tragedies. Over the summer of 1989, Tim's mother found out she had breast cancer. She was getting treatment when Hurricane Hugo swept through the Virgin Islands. The storm devastated the Duncans' island home. Tim's mother had to stop her treatment while the hospital was repaired.

Hurricane Hugo went on to hit Florida after slamming the Virgin Islands.

Hugo destroyed the pool where Tim's team had practiced, and many of the other pools on St. Croix. Afraid to practice in the ocean, Tim decided to take some time off from swimming. Then, the day before he turned 14, his mother died. Swimming had been part of Tim's bond with his mother. It was hard for him to think about going to a meet without her. He quit the sport for good.

Tim's family did their best to support him. They understood why he no longer wanted to swim. But they also knew Tim was a natural-born athlete. They hoped he would find another sport he could enjoy.

A LUCKY BREAK

Tim had joined his high school's basketball team, but he wasn't exactly a star. Ricky Lowery, Cheryl's husband, had played college basketball in the US. He decided to start working with Tim on the backyard hoop. Lowery found his brother-in-law a quick learner.

By the time Tim returned to school for his junior year, he had grown to nearly six foot nine (2 m). He played center, the position typically held by a team's

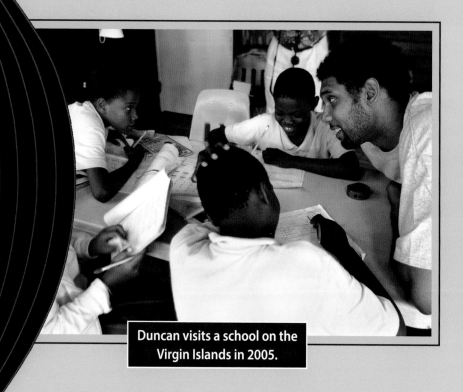

Duncan visits a school on the Virgin Islands in 2005.

HURRICANE HOOP

Cheryl and Ricky Lowery lived in Ohio when the hurricane hit. One year earlier, they had sent Tim a basketball hoop as a Christmas gift. When they returned to St. Croix, they were surprised to see the hoop still standing.

tallest players. Combining skilled ballhandling with his new size and strength, Tim became a force on the court.

After hearing about Tim, Dave Odom, the basketball coach at Wake Forest University in North Carolina, came to see him play. Odom was sold. He convinced Tim to come to Wake Forest once he finished his senior year.

Leaving his family and friends behind in St. Croix was tough for Tim. But he was excited to see what kind of future awaited him at Wake Forest. Still just 17, he agreed to join the Demon Deacons basketball team.

In his first college game, Tim didn't even attempt a shot. College teams played in a completely different style than he was used to. But he came roaring back in his next game, going double-double—double-digit numbers in both points and rebounds. It wasn't long before Tim was named the Atlantic Coast Conference's (ACC) Rookie of the Week. He was named Player of the Week three weeks later.

Duncan's college career was a huge success. From his sophomore year on, rumors spread that he would leave college early to join the NBA Draft. But Tim had promised

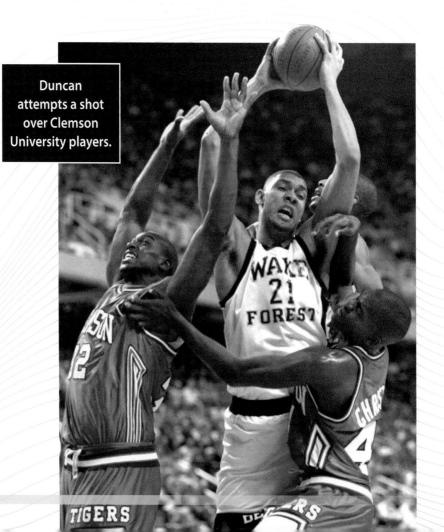

Duncan attempts a shot over Clemson University players.

Duncan makes a dunk in a game against Oklahoma State.

his mother he'd finish his schooling. So he stayed at Wake Forest, racking up ACC championships and individual awards. "I got stronger, smarter, and better prepared," he said.

Duncan earned his degree in psychology in 1997. He left college with a 97–31 record. He was a two-time ACC Player of the Year. He was the all-time leading shot blocker in ACC history and the all-time leading rebounder in National Collegiate Athletic Association history. He was also, finally, ready to enter the NBA Draft.

DOUBLE TROUBLE

The San Antonio Spurs drafted Duncan with the first pick in the first round. Going into the 1997–1998 season, Spurs coach Gregg Popovich had two great big men: Duncan and Robinson, the talented center. He wanted to use them together, but how?

Duncan and David Robinson in 1997

Robinson (*left*) and Duncan (*right*) were known for leaping up to block shots at the same time.

Years earlier, Duncan's brother-in-law had underestimated how tall Duncan would be. So he taught him the outside game. Duncan's range of abilities meant Popovich could use him as either a center or a power forward. Duncan and the equally flexible Robinson could play side by side.

Not only did Duncan and Robinson work well together, but they quickly became friends. The pair became known as the Twin Towers. Combined, they averaged 42 points and 24 rebounds a game during the first 32 games of the season. And Duncan was still improving. When Robinson sat out six games with an injury, Duncan boosted his averages to 25 points, 13 rebounds, and 4.5 blocked shots per game.

Duncan and Robinson stand with Cynthia Cooper of the Women's National Basketball Association in 1999.

TWO OF A KIND

Duncan was only the second player in NBA history to be named to the All-NBA First Team and All-Defensive Team in each of his first three seasons in the league. Can you guess the first? David Robinson!

After an amazing first season, Duncan was named NBA Rookie of the Year.

The Spurs had a slow start to the 1998–1999 season. But the slump didn't last, and soon they hit a winning streak. San Antonio made it to the playoffs, where they quickly knocked out the Minnesota Timberwolves. The Los Angeles Lakers had superstars Shaquille O'Neal and Kobe Bryant, but they too fell to Duncan and the Spurs. Duncan wouldn't be satisfied until he had an NBA Finals ring. Facing off against the New York Knicks, he and Robinson made it happen. Duncan was thrilled to win his first championship title and be named Finals MVP.

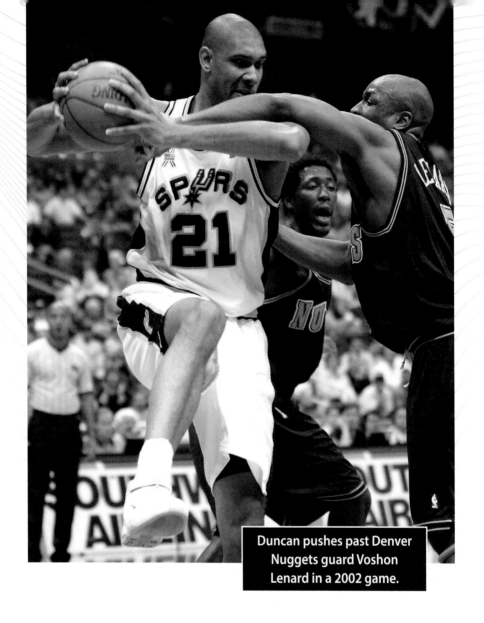

Duncan pushes past Denver Nuggets guard Voshon Lenard in a 2002 game.

The Twin Towers had a few great seasons left together. In 2002, Duncan won the league's MVP award. The following year, he won it again. He also won Finals MVP after leading the Spurs to their second NBA championship—Robinson's last.

Once Robinson retired in 2003, Duncan took on full leadership of the Spurs. His career as an NBA superstar was just getting started.

Duncan and Robinson hold their MVP and NBA championship trophies after beating the New Jersey Nets in the 2003 Finals.

SPURS SUPERSTAR

In 2005, Duncan led his team to their third championship title against the Detroit Pistons, scoring 25 points and 11 rebounds in a winner-take-all Game 7. He won his third

Duncan hoists another MVP trophy and NBA championship trophy in 2005.

Duncan on the move during Game 4 of the 2007 NBA Finals

NBA Finals MVP award for his performance. "His complete game is so sound, so fundamental," Popovich said. "[He] was the force that got it done for us."

The Spurs made it back to the playoffs the next two seasons, winning yet another title in 2007. Though the team then faced a string of challenging seasons, Duncan's play stayed strong. Even into his 30s, he was one of few players in the NBA averaging at least 20 points and 10 rebounds a game.

Duncan in Game 3 of the 2014 Western Conference Finals, against the Oklahoma City Thunder

AMONG THE GREATS

Including Duncan, only five players have won Finals MVP at least three times. Magic Johnson, Shaquille O'Neal, and LeBron James each have three Finals MVP awards. Michael Jordan has the most all-time with six.

With Duncan as their leader, the Spurs made the playoffs again and again. But the team wasn't destined for another championship until 2014. Duncan became the second player in history to win a title in three different decades.

At 38, he knew he was nearing the end of his career. He had experienced soreness in his right knee for years, and it sometimes caused him to miss games. In 2016, Duncan decided it was time to retire—from playing. He would become an assistant coach for the Spurs.

Duncan's 19 seasons with San Antonio are unmatched. The Spurs won five NBA championships and had a 1,072–438 regular season record, the best in the NBA. Duncan himself ranks among the top NBA players in points, rebounds, and blocks. Though he stepped down

Duncan listens while guests speak at his jersey retirement ceremony in 2016.

Duncan coaches Spurs forward DeMar DeRozan in March 2020.

from coaching in November 2020, he has an amazing legacy with the Spurs. In 2021, he was inducted into the Naismith Memorial Basketball Hall of Fame.

SIGNIFICANT STATS

NBA champion: 1999, 2003, 2005, 2007, 2014

NBA Finals MVP: 1999, 2003, 2005

NBA league MVP: 2002, 2003

Career blocks: 3,020 (fifth-all-time)

Career rebounds: 15,091 (sixth-all-time)

Career points: 26,496 (14th all-time)

GLOSSARY

assist: a pass that makes it possible for another player to score

block: to strike the ball to prevent a score

center: a basketball position that usually plays near the basket

foul: making an illegal move in a game

outside game: a play that takes place away from the basket

point guard: a basketball position that usually directs a team's offense

power forward: a basketball position that plays similarly to a center with more movement around the court

rebound: gaining possession of the ball after a missed shot

rookie: a first-year player

SOURCE NOTES

9   Ken Rappoport, *Tim Duncan: Star Forward* (Berkeley Heights, NJ: Enslow, 2000), 69.

15   John Albert Torres, *Sports Great Tim Duncan* (Berkeley Heights, NJ: Enslow, 2000), 18.

20   Tim Duncan, "NBA Champions," SlamDuncan.com, April 30, 2020, http://www.slamduncan.com/diary-champions.php.

23   "Spurs Dethrone Pistons to Take Third NBA Title," NBA.com, June 23, 2005, https://web.archive.org/web/20090219212308 /http://www.nba.com/games/20050623/DETSAS/recap.html.

LEARN MORE

Basketball Reference: Tim Duncan
https://www.basketball-reference.com/players/d/duncati01.html

Levit, Joe. *Basketball's G.O.A.T.: Michael Jordan, LeBron James, and More.* Minneapolis: Lerner Publications, 2020.

Monson, James. *Behind the Scenes Basketball.* Minneapolis: Lerner Publications, 2020.

NBA Advanced Stats: Tim Duncan
https://stats.nba.com/player/1495/

San Antonio Spurs
https://www.nba.com/spurs/

Ybarra, Andres. *Great Basketball Debates.* Minneapolis: Abdo, 2019.

INDEX

PHOTO ACKNOWLEDGMENTS

Image credits: AP Photo/John W. McDonough, p. 4; Pongnathee Kluaythong/EyeEm/
Getty Images, pp. 5, 28; AP Photo/Michael Conroy, p. 6; AP Photo/Mark Lennihan, p. 7;
Andrey Armyagov/Shutterstock.com, p. 8; US Air Force photo by Ken Hackman, p. 9;
National Oceanic and Atmospheric Administration (NOAA), p. 10; AP Photo/Andres
Leighton, p. 12; AP Photo/Bob Jordan, p. 14; AP Photo/Tom Pidgeon, p. 15; AP Photo/
David Zalubowski, p. 16; AP Photo/Joe Cavaretta, p. 17; AP Photo/Luca Bruno, p. 18; AP
Photo/Eric Gay, pp. 20, 21, 22, 23; AP Photo/Sue Ogrocki, p. 24; AP Photo/Darren Abate,
p. 26; AP Photo/Nell Redmond, p. 27.

Cover: Jed Jacobsohn/Getty Images, Christian Petersen/Getty Images.